Baker's 2nd Law: "The future of the Mexican Energy Sector is clear; it's only the present moment that is so confusing".[1]

INTRODUCTION

"El petróleo mexicano pertenece al pueblo mexicano"[2] Mexico's oil belongs to Mexico's people. For 73 years, Mexico has closely identified oil with their sovereignty. Mexico is one of the world's major oil producers and since the Cantarell Field started producing in 1978, it has been a major oil exporter. The days of easy oil are coming to a close due to the developed oil fields drying up and as Mexico enters its second decade of declining reserves, it runs the risk of becoming an oil importer in the next five to ten years. According to Pemex forecasts, oil production will decline by a projected 58% over this decade and with the Mexican economy so dependent on oil revenues, this will have serious implications on Mexico's fiscal policy.[3] Mexico is currently the third top exporter of oil to the United States, after Canada and Saudi Arabia, and the loss of this oil does have national security implications.[4] The United States demand for oil is still high and "since 1993 America has imported more oil than it produces and today roughly 60% of the oil used in the United States is imported."[5] It is far better for the US to have a steady source of oil coming from its southern border than relying on the likes of Hugo Chavez in Venezuela and politically unstable Nigeria. Mexico must enact critical reforms to its oil industry in order to prevent the nation from becoming a net oil importer by 2020.

I will examine the declining production of the current Mexican oil fields, examine their upstream issues with exploration and development, examine their downstream issues and how it

---

[1] George Baker, "Outlook for Mexican Oil and Gas: Policy, Commerce and Corporate Governance." *New York Energy Forum*, April 25, 2011, 7

[2] *Baker Institute Policy Report*, "The Future of Oil in Mexico," 1

[3] *Jane's Military and Security Assessments*, "Natural Resources," Feb 16, 2011,

[4] U.S. Energy Information Administration, Crude Oil and Petroleum Imports Top 15 Countries, 2011 Import Highlights, September 29, 2011

[5] David Bernreuther, "Building Alternative-Energy Partnerships With Latin America," *USAWC Strategy Research Project*, (2007)

financially impacts Pemex and finally examine Brazil and Norway and how their oil companies (Petrobras and Statoil) can provide a road map for Mexico.

Background

No discussion of the Mexican oil industry can begin without first understanding the importance of The Political Constitution of the United Mexican States and the events of March 18, 1938. The current Mexican Constitution was approved in February 1917 and Article 27 states, "The Nation owns what follows: all natural resources at both the continental platform and the islands' seafloor...all the oil and all solid, liquid and gaseous hydrocarbons."[6] After much labor unrest and foreign company resistance to the formation of unions, President Cárdenas expropriated the oil sector and evicted all the foreign oil companies. He cited Article 27 and ever since, the state, oil and populace of Mexico have all been intertwined. "In Mexico, the expropriation is viewed as a patriotic triumph, in which the federal government seized control of the country's most valuable natural resource."[7] This date is so important to the Mexican people that it is currently celebrated as a civic Mexican holiday. What was created in the place of the US and Anglo-Dutch companies, was the first of the major National Oil Companies (NOCs), Petróleos Mexicanos or Pemex.

Counter Arguments

It has been 73 years since Pemex became the national oil company and the Pemex green gas station and the idea of state oil have solidly been linked to Mexican sovereignty for all these years. "Many Mexicans have come to regard Pemex as a flagship of their national identity...loyalty to its icon has persisted...after all Pemex is not just a banner; it also embodies a

---

[6] Universidad Nacional Autonoma De Mexico, 2005
http://www.juridicas.unam.mx/infjur/leg/constmex/pdf/consting.pdf
[7] Noel Maurer, "The Empire Struck Back: The Mexican Oil Expropriation of 1938 Reconsidered," *Harvard Business School*, June 30, 2010, http://www.hbs.edu/research/pdf/10-108.pdf

hope for future security and prosperity."[8] Ernesto Marcos, former CEO of Pemex, recently stated "(Pemex) is synonymous with the ultimate symbol of Mexican cultural identity: the Virgin of Guadalupe. The nationalization of petroleum is closely tied to our identity as a country and our sovereignty as an independent nation. It is almost a religious myth, an object of devotion."[9] Against this backdrop, it is no surprise that all three of the political parties in Mexico acknowledge some sort of reform is needed, but not so far as to recommend a change in the constitution. The Mexican public believes that a public company will work for the good of the people while a private company will only benefit the wealthy, and the foreign companies that want to revenge 1938 and take from the Mexican people what is rightfully theirs.

The James A. Baker, III Institute for Public Policy did a study showing that declining oil revenues will not have a shock effect on economic growth as predicted by some. In 2008, oil revenues represented 37% of the public sector revenues or about 8.7% of the Mexican GDP.[10] Mexico's Ministry of Energy outlook to 2017 has oil production of crude staying at a level of 2.9 million barrels per day. It is also projected that GDP grows at an average rate of 3% per year for the next nine years, and that the price of oil will remain on average at US$70 per barrel for the rest of the decade. While the percentage of oil revenues will drop from 36.9% to 28.6% in this study, the effect of this will result in a "real depreciation of the peso that will have beneficial effects on the competitiveness of non-oil exports, as well as on the profitability of, and investment in, the tradable goods sector."[11] This will then compensate for the fall in oil reserves

---

[8] George Baker, "Outlook for Mexican Oil and Gas: Policy, Commerce and Corporate Governance." *New York Energy Forum*, April 25, 2011, 7.
[9] Megan Lan, Silva Marcelo and Weber Renzo, "The Mexican Oil Dilemma: Refining Pemex," *The Wharton School of the University of Pennsylvania* (April 20, 2009)
[10] Jaime Ros, "The Macroeconomic Consequences of Falling Oil Revenues in Mexico: A Looming Crisis or a Mixed Blessing?" *The Future of Oil in Mexico*. April 29, 2011: 10
[11] Ibid: 19

and exports. Plus this projection finds that oil will decline gradually and that will buy time for the Mexican government to adjust rather than face a sudden fiscal crisis.

Main Body

The nationalization of oil was supposed to lead the Mexican people to prosperity. To the Mexican government, the foreigners were gone and "El petroleo es nuestro" or the oil is ours. Sadly however the great oil fields are drying up and the company is not positioned to thrive in the future given its current make-up. "For Pemex, being used as the government's golden goose means the company can't be run as a real oil company. There is not enough money left for oil exploration, exploitation and processing. Plus, Pemex's leaders are not chosen for their expertise in the petroleum industry, but their political connections."[12]

Currently, Mexico is pumping oil from two major locations; the Sureste Basin in the shallow waters of the Gulf of Mexico and from the coastal onshore Tampico-Misantla Basin. The existing reserves in both of these locations are running low and unfortunately there has been little upstream activity to find new fields to replace the aging workhorses of the past several decades.

Discovered in 1976 in the shallow waters in the Bay of Campeche north of Tabasco in the Sureste Basin by a fisherman whose nets became clogged with the floating oil, the Cantarell Oil Field has been the engine driving the Mexican oil production for the past 35 years. Cantarell at one time was the second largest producing oil field in the world.[13] Mexico currently ranks seventh in the world for production of crude oil, but only 17th in the world in oil reserves.[14] "The obvious consequence of high rates of production but low reserves is that the reserves will not last

---

[12] Allan Wall, "PEMEX Fritters Away Mexico's Oil Wealth. Closing The Borders Would Help," *Memo from Mexico, V-Dare.com*, May 1, 2008., http://www.vdare.com/articles/memo-from-mexico-by-allan-wall-61
[13] G.R. Morton, "Cantarell, The Second Largest Oil Field in the World is Dying," *Energy Bulletin*, Aug 18, 2004:1
[14] Manik Talwani, PhD, "Oil and Gas in Mexico: Geology, Production Rates and Reserves," *The Future of Oil in Mexico*, (April 11): 10

4

very long."[15] At one time Mexico was pumping 2.1 million barrels a day out of the ground at Cantarell. Today that number is about 400,000. Production at Cantarell has been declining since 2004 and Mexico's oil reserves have declined for the past 12 consecutive years. The six year time span from 2004 to 2010 shows this steep decline "from a peak of 2.136 million barrels per day (b/d) in 2004 to only 685,000 b/d in 2009 and 558,000 b/d in 2010."[16] Another way to look at this is in 2004, Cantarell contributed 62 percent of Mexico's total crude oil production while in 2008 the total was only 24 percent.[17]

The geological structure of the Sureste Basin is such that Cantarell is a highly pressurized oil field. To keep the flow of oil coming and their exports high, Pemex drilled and drilled and drilled into the highly pressurized ocean floor. When the flow began to slow due to the loss of pressure because of all the wells, Pemex began pumping nitrogen into Cantarell to boost up the pressure and increase outflow. The nitrogen worked for a time, but continued injection is likely to damage productivity.[18]

In order to make-up for the losses of Cantarell, Pemex has been focusing on a nearby production field in the Sureste Basin. The Ku-Maloob-Zaap (KMZ) field is located near the Cantarell Field and it currently is producing more than Cantarell at 808,000 barrels a day; about 500,000 b/d higher than its 2004 levels.[19] This field has also required nitrogen injects to keep the production rate up in 2009. This field was discovered in 1979 and has been the most productive find for Pemex since the Cantarell find. A major issue with KMZ is the heavy oil that it produces. "Heavy oil also often contains large amounts of sulfur and metals...which are most

[15] Talwani, "Oil and Gas in Mexico":10
[16] Peter Hartley, PhD and Kenneth Medlock, PhD. "The Revenue Efficiency of Pemex: A Comparative Approach." *The Future of Oil in Mexico*. April 29, 2011: 15
[17] Jane's "Natural Resources"
[18] *The Oil Drum*, "Cantarell's loss is Ku-Maloob-Zaap's (KMZ) gain," Feb 7, 2007, http://www.theoildrum.com/node/2247
[19] Hartley and Medlock, "The Revenue Efficiency of Pemex,": 15

undesirable from a refiner's point of view."[20] Some argue that KMZ will likely start its decline, like that of Cantarell, this year or next and "internal Pemex documents indicate that KMZ is producing increasingly large quantities of water along with oil-a sign that the aging field may have already peaked."[21]

The Tampico Misantla Basin contains both old oil fields and prospective fields. Pemex has been drilling in the Golden lane for years with both the Cerro Azul No. 4 and Poza Rica fields as historical productive producers. What is important about this Basin is the potential of the Chicontepec Field. These deposits are believed to be rivaling those of Saudi Arabia, but so far, the recovery rate has been very low with a forecast of only 70,000 b/d in 2011.[22] There are problems with this field as it is spread out over 2,400 square miles, consists of 29 separate deposits and is under low pressure. Because of the rock formation where the oil is located it is difficult to drill in and with the low pressure of the field, the use of current enhanced oil recovery (EOR) techniques is difficult to apply. New techniques will need to be developed and right now, it will be years before an effective use of this field will occur.[23] It is expected that this field has reserves of 15 billion barrels and since the Vicente Fox administration, Mexico has made it a point of effort to develop this field. However, some critics say that Chicontepec is a "hallmark of the distorted perception of reality that pervades the government."[24] The graph below shows the output relationship between the current oil fields in production.

[20] Talwani, "Oil and Gas in Mexico":24

[21] Elliott Gue, "Down Mexico Way: Oil and Politics South of the Border," *Seeking Alpha,* January 5, 2010, http://seekingalpha.com/article/180916-down-mexico-way-oil-and-politics-south-of-the-border

[22] Hartley and Medlock, "The Revenue Efficiency of Pemex,": 15

[23] Talwani, "Oil and Gas in Mexico": 16

[24] Jasmina Kelemen, "A Band-aid Approach," *ICIS Chemical Business*, Sep 7, 2009, http://www.icis.com/Articles/2009/09/07/9243874/mexicos-pemex-seeks-to-stem-the-decline-in-oil-production.html

Unfortunately, the Mexican government did not create a viable company post-Cantarell, instead, "the state acted as a leach: the federal government…relies on Pemex for close to 40 percent of its operating budget. This amounts to nearly 60 percent of the company's revenues being siphoned off every year."[26] Also, Pemex's annual budget is established by the government and there is no flexibility to change due to unforeseen conditions. When the price of oil drops or pipelines are ruptured, Pemex suffers.[27] While Cantarell was pumping 2 million barrels of oil a day out of the ocean, it was easy to overlook these extravagant numbers. When oil prices were high, it was easy for the government to milk the cash cow while the going was good. Now that the peak production has passed, it is apparent to see that Pemex is suffering from the lack of money put into its ability to reach deep water oil, refinery capabilities and technologies like saltwater extraction and sub-surface drilling as discussed earlier. In addition to the revenue siphoning that occurs at the federal government level, Pemex as a NOC has other handicaps that it faces with declining oil production.

[25] "Investor Relations," *Pemex*, March 8, 2011, http://contratos.pemex.com/portal/files/content/20110308cmg.pdf.
[26] Patrick Corcoran, "Mexico's Pemex Struggles to Overcome Years of Mismanagement." *Bertelsmann Stiftung* , Sept 8, 2011, http://futurechallenges.org/local/mexicos-pemex-struggles-to-overcome-years-of-mismanagement
[27] Hartley and Medlock, "The Revenue Efficiency of Pemex ,": 17

When examining the technical efficiency of Pemex, high employment robs the company of capital better used elsewhere. In the Hartley and Medlock theoretical model, Pemex was compared with other NOCs and it ranked 35th out of the 62 firms in its sample.[28] One of the areas viewed was employment. In 2008, Pemex had 139,787 employees. In comparison, Statoil Hydro, the NOC of Norway had 49,439 employees and Saudi Aramco, the NOC of Saudi Arabia had 53,475 employees. When evaluating the revenue per employee, Pemex came in at .585, Statoil at 1.85 and Saudi Aramco at 3.28. In this comparison, Pemex ranked 52nd out of 62 NOCs.[29] A companion research project by Eller, Hartley and Medlock in 2007 bears this out as well:

Company	Revenue per Employee $/employee	Government Ownership %	Country
Pemex	506	100%	Mexico
Saudi Aramco	2,261	100%	Saudi Arabia
Statoil	1,910	71%	Norway

This backs up the conclusion that "there is strong evidence of over-employment by Pemex and the analysis suggests that Pemex would have been able to earn more than 48% additional revenue…by more efficiently employing the resources at its disposal."[31] This large employee figure also means it has a powerful union and a large retiree force with approximately 70,000 retired Pemex workers[32] drawing off a pension fund worth about US$34 billion.[33] From just 2000-2002 data, Pemex had to dedicate 55% of net sales to fund these large payrolls.[34] Lack of available money for investment in the upstream sector of Pemex is but one of the problems

[28] Hartley and Medlock, "The Revenue Efficiency of Pemex ,": 12
[29] Ibid: 18
[30] Stacey Eller, Peter Hartley, and Kenneth Medlock, "Empirical Evidence on the Operational Efficiency of National Oil Companies," *The James A. Baker, III Institute for Public Policy, Rice University,* 2007: 11 http://www.rice.edu/energy/publications/docs/NOCs/Papers/NOC_Empirical.pdf
[31] Hartley and Medlock, "The Revenue Efficiency of Pemex,": 12
[32] Andrew Smolski, "PEMEX and the long road to privatization." *Oilprice.com,* July 20, 2011
[33] Hartley and Medlock, "The Revenue Efficiency of Pemex,": 18
[34] Ibid: 18

facing the company. Declining production and rising demand within the country are at a crossroads for Mexico's upstream sector.

For Pemex, the major question is where are the prospective oil reserves? According to Pemex's General Director Office, almost 30 billion of the projected 52 billion barrels of oil resides in the deep and ultra-deep water of the Gulf of Mexico.[35]   As the below picture visualizes, there are over 300 deep water wells in the US part of the Gulf while "Pemex has drilled just ten deep water wells, but found little oil. It lacks the expertise, technology and capital it needs."[36]

[37]

Deep water drilling is not something that Pemex has a history of and upwards of 90% of their drilling to date has been in water 100 meters or less.[38] So where does this deep water expertise lie? Mostly in the private companies still called "Big Oil." Because most of the cheap, easy to

---

[35] Gerardo Bazan, and Cristobal Gonzalez, "Mexican Oil Industry: Shifting to Difficult Oil," *General Director Office, Petroeos Mexicanos,* Sept 19, 2011: 4 www.worldenergy.org/documents/congresspapers/386.pdf.
[36] "How many Mexicans does it take to drill an oil well?" *The Economist,* October 1, 2009, http://www.economist.com/node/14548839
[37] http://www.nationalgeographic.com/educator-resources/oil-spills/map/gulf-oil/
[38] George Baker, "Mexico faces challenges in deepwater operations," *Oil & Gas Journal,* Nov 22, 2004: 19

access oil in the world is controlled by NOCs (Saudi Arabia, Russia, Venezuela and Iran), the

Big Oil companies or International Oil Companies (IOCs) like BP, Chevron, ExxonMobil, RD

Shell, et al "have to push the limits of technology in exploration and extraction (because) they

have no other option remaining."[39] This is where the constitutional restraints put on Pemex

affect the company's ability to work with these IOCs to get to the oil. While the Mexican

Constitution prohibits IOCs from owning any Mexican oil, it has allowed Pemex to work with

foreign companies to drill for oil. These service contracts allow subcontractors to partner with

Pemex for a flat fee. Oil service companies like Halliburton or Schlumberger have been

assisting Pemex in shallow water or onshore drilling for a flat fee. However, "the major

exploration and production companies largely stayed away as they weren't allowed to absorb any

of the upside from rising oil prices."[40] With these service contracts, there is no incentive for the

IOCs to take the financial risks needed to explore and drill in deep water. The IOCs want to

engage in a incentive-based contract where they share the profits of the oil by the barrel. The

state continues to own the oil that is pumped from the ground, but the company is paid a fee for

each barrel they pump. The IOCs in turn pick up a share of the cost to find and extract the oil.[41]

A 2010 Mexican Supreme Court ruling found that Pemex could start to make these incentive-

based contracts, but is it enough to entice the big IOCs to make a commitment in the Gulf of

Mexico? The issue for the IOCs is that they still will not own the oil and count it against their

reserves. This in turn is a "major drawback since oil companies are judged by the public markets

in large part by their ability to replace their reserves."[42] They need this oil to compensate for the

---

[39] Philip Bethge, Alexander Jung, Nils Klawitter, and Renate Nimitz-Koester, "Does Deep Sea Drilling Have a Future?" *Spiegel Online International* , May 13, 2010,
http://www.spiegel.de/international/business/0,1518,694346,00.html
[40] Cyrus Sanati, "Mexican oil may not be worth it," *CNNMoney*, Dec 9, 2010,
http://money.cnn.com/2010/12/09/news/international/Mexico_oil.fortune/index.htm
[41] Ibid
[42] Sanati, "Mexican oil may not be worth it."

high costs of deep water drilling. In 2007, one Chevron deep water exploration rig costs US$500,000 a day to run and Chevron has several of these operating every day in the Gulf of Mexico. Chevron's deep water exploration division alone has an annual budget of US$1billion.[43] The same year, IOCs alone spent over US$5 billion to discover reserves in just one field in the Gulf of Mexico.[44] With the needed technology, high financial costs to explore, drill, and recover deep water oil, it is vital that Pemex partner with IOCs like Chevron. "Mexico needs to permit outside, independent oil companies to participate as partners in exploration and development. That means to share the risks and rewards. In other words, Mexico should leverage foreign capital and technology, while sharing the eventual oil production in an equitable manner."[45] Another problem facing Pemex is the drilling of IOCs in US waters that border Mexican waters. A recent "BP discovery of its large oil find in the Gulf of Mexico was cause for concern to Mexican officials because of a 'drinking straw' effect (that) might occur."[46] Mexican oil might belong to the Mexican people, but it might ultimately end up in British Petroleum drilling rigs.

In addition to upstream issues of exploring and extracting oil, Pemex has a downstream issue with refining their oil and keeping revenue within the company/country. "Despite having the fourth largest proven crude reserves in the western hemisphere, Mexico imports more than a quarter of its oil products, a situation that stems from Pemex's failure to add refining capacity along with growing domestic demand for fuel."[47] Currently Mexico operates just six refineries.

---

[43] Amanda Little, "Pumped Up: Chevron Drills Down 30,000 Feet to Tap Oil-Rich Gulf of Mexico," Wired, Aug 21, 2007, http://www.wired.com/cars/energy/magazine/15-09/mf_jackrig?currentPage=all
[44] Ibid
[45] Byron King, "Mexico's Crashing Oil Industry," *WhiskeyandGunpowder.com* , Aug 9, 2010, http://whiskeyandgunpowder.com/mexicos-crashing-oil-industry/
[46] Nancy Cruz, "Mexico: An Oil Nation in Crisis," *Council on Hemispheric Affairs*, Oct 22, 2009: 6, http://www.coha.org/mexico-an-oil-nation-in-crisis/
[47] "Pemex Looks At US Refining Market As Domestic Gasoline Demand Surges," *Penn* Energy, March 1, 2011, http://www.pennenergy.com/index/articles/newsdisplay/1376607740.html

In comparison, the United States operates 148 and the state of Alaska alone has six.[48] According to Mexican government projections, "Mexico will need to build a new refinery every three to four years over the next two decades to meet growing domestic demand for oil products."[49] Currently, only one refinery is planned (the Tula refinery scheduled to come online in 2015) and Mexico has not built a refinery since 1979. Mexico's downstream sector has "remained virtually stagnant while domestic consumption of refined oil products has grown at an average annual rate of 3.4% between 1980 and 2008."[50] Because of this, even though Mexico is an oil exporting nation, it has a higher dependency on imported oil products (22%) than its NAFTA partners Canada (12.4%) and the United States (9.23%).[51] In 2007 for example, Mexico imported 366,000 barrels of gasoline accounting for 46% of their demand.[52] Compounding the problems, Pemex faces an aging pipeline infrastructure that is inadequate, forcing the company to rely on trucks to move petroleum which adds additional costs. Further compounding the problem for Pemex is the years of underinvestment now have created an issue where they need to invest in their downstream sector while they have even greater issues with oil production. It will cost Pemex $13 billion to build the new refinery and overhaul an existing one and some critics argue that they have better use for those billions.[53] Money desperately needed for deep water exploration and drilling will be siphoned off to fix their refining shortfalls.

Finally, another area in the downstream sector that is hurting Pemex financially is the government subsidy for gasoline. For the first quarter of 2011, Subsidies were US$2.28 billion,

[48] US Dept of Energy "Petroleum & Other Liquids" June 24, 2011,
http://www.eia.gov/dnav/pet/pet_pnp_cap1_dcu_nus_a.htm
[49] "Pemex Looks At US Refining Market As Domestic Gasoline Demand Surges"
[50] Carlos Dominguez,"Beyond Efficiency: The Politics of Investment Policies in the Oil Industry," *The Future of Oil in Mexico*. April 29, 2011: 10
[51] Ibid: 12
[52] "Pemex Looks At US Refining Market As Domestic Gasoline Demand Surges"
[53] Robert Campbell, "UPDATE 1-Mexico eyes US, European refineries for supply." *Reuters*, May 12, 2010

"roughly the same amount budgeted by the finance ministry for subsidies in the entire year."[54] In 2008, "according to official numbers from the 2008 Mexican government's budget, the subsidy to gasoline and diesel in 2008 amounts to 2.4% of the country's Gross Domestic Product (GDP)."[55] Even the Mexican government acknowledges that there are issues with the growing revenue that Mexico is dedicating to subsidizing gasoline. But with elections upcoming, there will be a hesitation to raise the price of gasoline as "both rival PRI and PRD parties would surely lambast Calderón's PAN party administration over the higher gasoline prices to score political points, as they have in the past."[56] The bottom line is that state run Pemex has its gasoline prices set by the government. If Mexico was a free-market economy like the US and gas prices were set by the market, "the federal government would have to have to reduce its dependence on this revenue. At the same time, these companies would have to be more efficient, to allow them to be competitive in the market, which they are currently not."[57] This lack of efficiency hurts Pemex in the upstream sector in exploring deep water, in the downstream sector in refining oil and in the loss of revenue that could be better spent elsewhere. Critics of these subsidies say "the government is squandering profits from high crude prices just when it should be spending them on projects like… refineries and oil platforms."[58] Pemex is struggling with their dwindling reserves and production, their lack of deep water drilling abilities and the competing requirements within the company between the downstream and upstream sectors. There are two fellow national oil companies whom Mexico could look to for best practices in righting the listing ship of Pemex.

---

[54] David Biller, "Govt to look to lower gasoline subsidies in 1H11 - Eurasia – Mexico," *Oil & Gas*, April 1, 2011, http://www.bnamericas.com/news/oilandgas/govt-to-look-to-lower-gasoline-subsidies-in-1h11-eurasia
[55] Armenta Fraire Leticia, interview by *Watch Subsidy*, "Breaking the cycle: Subsidies for transport fuels in Mexico ," *Global Subsidies Initiative*, Nov 11, 2008
[56] Biller, "Govt to look to lower gasoline subsidies in 1H11 - Eurasia – Mexico"
[57] Leticia, "Breaking the cycle: Subsidies for transport fuels in Mexico."
[58] Michael O'Boyle, and Noel Randewich, "Mexico takes economic gamble to keep fuel cheap," *Reuters*, May 29, 2008, http://www.reuters.com/article/2008/05/29/us-mexico-economy-idUSN2944639820080529

As the Woodrow Wilson International Center for Scholars pointed out in 2010, "the story of the oil industry in Latin America in recent years has been one of both highs and lows, with positive news coming out of countries such as Brazil…and less encouraging developments taking place in Mexico."[59] In 1980, Brazil was an oil importing nation with 77 percent of its oil requirements coming from outside its country. Now, it is an oil exporting nation with zero percent of its oil needs imported. And since 1980, it has increased its oil production by 876 percent![60] Even though it is a NOC, Petrobras is a government controlled, but publicly traded oil company.

Like Mexico, Brazil kicked out the foreign oil companies in 1964 and created Petrobras, an oil monopoly; they even had a similar battle cry in, "O Petroleo e Nosso" – "the Petroleum is ours!"[61] What is different is that in the 1970s, Brazil put energy security over resource nationalism and authorized risk contracts for IOCs, breaking the monopoly over exploration and production. Brazil and Petrobras went through several legal upheavals in the 1980 and 1990s but by 1997 the Petroleum Law was passed which allowed for non-state investment and authorized Petrobras to seek partial privatization. Although the government still contains overall control of the company, the introduction of competition to the company provided the needed stimulus for the NOC, something Pemex does not have.[62] As the below figure shows, IOCs from six countries are teamed-up with Petrobras in Brazilian oil production.

[59] Duncan Wood, "The Outlook for Energy Reform in Latin America," *Woodrow Wilson International Center for Scholars* , March 2010, http://www.wilsoncenter.org/publication/the-outlook-for-energy-reform-latin-america
[60] Bill Costello, "Import Brazil's Oil Policy, Not Brazil's Oil." *American Thinker*, April 10, 2011, http://www.americanthinker.com/2011/04/import_brazils_oil_policy_not.html
[61] David Mares PhD, "Oil Policy Reform in Resource Nationalist States: Lessons for Mexico." *The Future of Oil in Mexico*. April 29, 2011: 26, http://bakerinstitute.org/publications/EF-pub-MaresLessons-04292011.pdf
[62] Ibid, 29

This contract system with IOCs also allowed Petrobras to move into product sharing in the exploration and production in deep water. Prior to the 1997 law, Brazil was primarily a refining nation from oil imports, now it produces a quarter of the world's deep water oil and is scheduled to overtake Exxon as the leader in barrel reserves.[63] Petrobras also has the needed capital that Pemex does not have. When Petrobras went public in 2010, the initial public offering brought $67 billion to the company. "The share sale is an important part of the company's plans to double output over the next decade; it says it will spend $224 billion on offshore exploration and drilling…it is well-placed now to develop recently discovered oil fields off the Brazilian coast, including the Tupi fields, the largest discovery in the Americas in three decades."[64] Petrobras is also investing heavily in the necessary equipment to get after the deep water oil. It owns 14 ultra-deep water drilling rigs and by 2012 it will have added another 20 rigs that it is having built

[63] Brian O'Keefe and Doris Burke, "Petrobras: The next oil colossus," *CNNMoney*, March 8, 2011, http://features.blogs.fortune.cnn.com/2011/03/08/petrobras-the-next-oil-colossus/
[64] Julie Triedman, "Petrobras Stock Offering Raises $67 Billion, Setting New Record ." *The Am Law Daily*, Sept 24, 2010.

in Asia. The major Asian shipyards are full with shipbuilding orders, so they have now awarded contracts to Brazilian firms to supply another 28 rigs in 2014.[65] In comparison, Pemex hopes to have four deep water rigs drilling by 2012.[66] Petrobras's success is also due to their effort to tackle the challenges of deep water drilling. "This genuine effort at developing internal technological competencies has allowed Petrobras to extract the full potential from cooperative R&D to gain access to the new subsea boosting technology."[67] Partnership with industry leaders, infusion of capital, and competitiveness in the marketplace has thrust Petrobras into being a global bellwether for oil production.

Like Mexico and Brazil, Norway also has an oil law. The Norwegian government in 1963 established that "the ocean floor and the underground of the underwater areas off the coast of the Kingdom of Norway are under Norwegian sovereignty as regards the exploitation and research of natural deposits."[68] However, the major difference is that Norway had no foreign oil companies to expropriate in 1963. With limited oil expertise and limited means of investment, Norway had to reach out to IOCs. In 1971, Esso and Shell discovered the giant Brent oil field on the British side of their sea boundary with Norway. Statoil made the assumption that there were high probabilities of finding oil on the Norwegian side, so that they entered into contracts with Esso, Shell, Conoco and Mobil to explore. Statoil received 50% of the ownership share while the four IOCs split the rest.[69] This strategic alliance with the IOCs and Statoil's desire to secure "positions at each stage of the oil process, from upstream prospecting and production down to

[65] O'Keefe, "Petrobras: The next oil colossus,"
[66] Robert Campbell, "Mexico unveils new deepwater oil drilling rules." *Reuters*, January 11, 2011, http://www.reuters.com/article/2011/01/11/us-mexico-oil-idUSTRE70A6R320110111
[67] Andrea Goldstein, "The Emergence of Multilatinas: The Petrobras Experience." *Universia Business Review*, 2010, 103
[68] Helge Ryggvik, "The Norwegian Oil Experience: A toolbox for managing resources?" *Oslo: University of Oslo*, 2010 :16, http://www.sv.uio.no/tik/forskning/publikasjoner/tik-artikkelserie/Ryggvik.pdf
[69] Ibid: 31

refining, the chemical industry and the sale of oil products"[70] was only part of the equation. Statoil also knew it had to develop its technical know-how to compete with the big IOCs. It partnered with the geology departments at the Universities of Oslo and Bergen and found oil industry executives in the United States for the branches of the company.[71] Statoil is an industry leader because the company leadership had "the strategic aim of establishing a fully integrated oil company with independent positions at all stages of the production chain."[72] In addition, Pemex has a lot to learn from Norway in how it disperses part of its revenue to the Petroleum Fund of Norway, worth $147 billion. Norway "viewed oil revenues as a temporary, collective owned windfall that, instead of spurring consumption today, can be used to insulate the country from the storms of the global economy."[73] While Mexico spends revenue on gasoline subsidies, Norway spends revenue for a financial shock absorber and will use revenue and appreciation to spread the wealth of North Sea oil across several generations.[74]

Finally, the World Economic Forum in its Global Competitiveness Report 2009 evaluated 134 countries using 2007 data. "Both in the report and in off-line discussions with The Mexican Competitiveness Institute (IMCO) officials, the two countries that are recommended as ones that Mexico should emulate in upstream policy are Brazil and Norway."[75] Some results: for capacity for innovation, Mexico was ranked 67th, Brazil 27th and Norway 13th. For corporate boards, Mexico was ranked 82nd, Brazil 42nd and Norway 9th. Finally for overall percentile rankings, Mexico was in the 40th percentile, Brazil in the 63rd and Norway in the 87th. For government

---

[70] Ryggvik "The Norwegian Oil Experience: A toolbox for managing resources?": 41
[71] Ibid: 42
[72] Ibid: 47
[73] Daniel Gross, "Norway vs. the Oil Curse," *Slate*, October 29, 2004,
http://www.slate.com/articles/business/moneybox/2004/10/avoiding_the_oil_curse.html
[74] Ibid
[75] George Baker, "Mexico, Brazil, Norway upstream readiness weighed." *Oil & Gas Journal*, Aug 10, 2009,
http://www.ogj.com/articles/print/volume-107/issue-30/Exploration___Development/mexico-brazil-norway-upstream-readiness-weighed.html

effectiveness and innovation especially in the upstream area, these findings clearly show that Mexico is lagging behind other oil producing countries.[76]

Conclusions and Recommendations

Today, Mexico has a reserve of approximately 44 billion barrels of oil. "The volume…is approximately the same as the total for hydrocarbons produced in the country for more than 100 years."[77] These are primarily in the Chicontepec, Cantarell and KMZ fields. They also have prospective resources estimated at 52 billion barrels in the Gulf of Mexico.[78] The challenge for Pemex and Mexico is getting those reserves. "Given (Pemex's) relative inexperience in the sector, considerable foreign expertise will likely be needed, especially in key areas such as deep water drilling, subsea hardware and floating production systems."[79] In order to do this, significant reforms are necessary for Mexico to remain an oil exporting nation. Following the experiences of both Brazil and Norway in adapting their monopolistic oil companies, Mexico should amend their laws to allow Pemex to fully partner with Petrobras or Statoil from the NOC side or IOCs like Chevron, BP and RD Shell. Pemex cannot wait the years it will take for it to exploit its deep water reserves on its own. By partnering with proven deep water explorers like Petrobras who also brings the much needed equipment and technological expertise, Pemex could begin reversing their decade long trend of declining reserves. President Calderon "himself has stressed that Petrobras is a model for Pemex, stating that it is paradoxical that Petrobras is drilling ten thousand feet deep in the Gulf of Mexico (in US waters), while Mexico only has the organizational and operational capacity to drill three thousand feet."[80] Brazil has shown an

---

[76] Baker, "Mexico, Brazil, Norway upstream readiness weighed."
[77] (Bazan, "Mexican Oil Industry: Shifting to Difficult Oil," :2
[78] Ibid: 4
[79] Scott Weedan, "Mexico Seeks Reserves in Deepwater Gulf," *E&P*, Aug 15, 2011, http://www.epmag.com/2011/August/item87111.php
[80] Wood, "The Outlook for Energy Reform in Latin America," :6

interest in partnering with Mexico in oil exploration and with Pemex's heavy oil expertise and Petrobras's deep water drilling expertise; it could be a union to benefit both Latin American countries.

Pemex needs to begin deep water drilling now or Mexican oil will end up in the coffers of the United States. The 2000 US-Mexico agreement to hold off on exploration of the Gulf of Mexico border area expired in 2010 and it is only a matter of time before the US begins drilling. "Depending on the geological formation, some of that oil may be sucked over to the American side and lost to Mexico permanently; all because Mexico won't allow foreign investment."[81] Or as the Financial Times recently pointed out to its readers, "as long as 'made in Mexico' rules, you are going to exclude the interest of most oil companies."[82]

Pemex needs to have leaders that understand the oil industry, not just political appointees and they need to keep larger portions of their revenue so they can fix their downstream issues and dedicate money to their upstream exploration.

Remaining an oil exporting nation is vital for Mexico as "a shift towards oil importer status would be a severe burden on the Mexican government and curb its ability to provide important services, both related to social programs and internal peace and security."[83]

In the 2008 US Presidential Campaign, "Drill Baby Drill" became a rallying cry for the US to become self-sufficient in oil and reduce the imports from the Middle East. Recent US energy policy shows that its future unfortunately lies as an oil importing nation. Mexico's oil future lies in the oil-rich deep water of the Gulf of Mexico. Mexico has been a major exporter to the United States and with internal reforms within Pemex & legal changes to allow them to enter

---

[81] Wall, "PEMEX Fritters Away Mexico's Oil Wealth. Closing The Borders Would Help,"
[82] Adam Thomson, "Pemex issues private oil-production contracts," *Financial* Times, Aug 18, 2011, http://www.ft.com/cms/s/0/959c20ca-c9d2-11e0-b88b-00144feabdc0.html#axzz1bdP2n3Gb
[83] *Baker Institute Policy Report* , "The Future of Oil in Mexico," 1

into meaningful relationships with other oil companies they will continue to be a vital exporter of oil to the US.

BIBLIOGRAPHY

Baker, George, "Mexico faces challenges in deep water operations." Oil & Gas Journal, Nov 22, 2004, http://www.ogj.com/articles/print/volume-102/issue-44/general-interest/mexico-faces-challenges-in-deepwater-operations.html

Baker, George, "Mexico, Brazil, Norway upstream readiness weighed," *Oil & Gas Journal*, Aug 10, 2009, http://www.ogj.com/articles/print/volume-107/issue-30/Exploration___Development/mexico-brazil-norway-upstream-readiness-weighed.html

Baker, George, "Outlook for Mexican Oil and Gas: Policy, Commerce and Corporate Governance." *New York Energy Forum*, April 25, 2011, Accessed September 19, 2011, http://www.nyenergyforum.org/app/

Baker Institute Policy Report, "The Future of Oil in Mexico," No. 48, June, 2011, http://bakerinstitute.org/programs/energy-forum/publications/energy-studies/the-future-of-oil-in-mexico-el-futuro-del-sector-petrolero-en-mexico

Bazan, Gerardo, and Cristobal Gonzalez, General Director Office, Petroeos Mexicanos, "Mexican Oil Industry: Shifting to Difficult Oil," Accessed September 19, 2011. www.worldenergy.org/documents/congresspapers/386.pdf.

Bernreuther, David, "Building Alternative-Energy Partnerships with Latin America," *USAWC Strategy Research Project*, March 30, 2007, http://www.dtic.mil/cgi-bin/GetTRDoc?Location=U2&doc=GetTRDoc.pdf&AD=ADA469121

Bethge, Philip, Alexander Jung, Nils Klawitter, and Renate Nimitz-Koester, "Does Deep Sea Drilling Have a Future?" *Spiegel Online International*, May 13, 2010, http://www.spiegel.de/international/business/0,1518,694346,00.html

Biller, David, "Gov't to look to lower gasoline subsidies in 1H11 - Eurasia – Mexico," Oil & Gas, April 1, 2011, http://www.bnamericas.com/news/oilandgas/govt-to-look-to-lower-gasoline-subsidies-in-1h11-eurasia

Campbell, Robert, "UPDATE 1-Mexico eyes US, European refineries for supply," *Reuters*, May 12, 2010, http://www.reuters.com/article/2010/05/12/mexico-oil-refining-idUSN1224049020100512

Campbell, Robert, "Mexico unveils new deepwater oil drilling rules," *Reuters*, January 11, 2011, http://www.reuters.com/article/2011/01/11/us-mexico-oil-idUSTRE70A6R320110111

Corcoran, Patrick. Bertelsmann Stiftung, "Mexico's Pemex Struggles to Overcome Years of Mismanagement," Sept 8, 2011, http://futurechallenges.org/local/mexicos-pemex-struggles-to-overcome-years-of-mismanagement/

Costello, Bill, "Import Brazil's Oil Policy, Not Brazil's Oil," *American Thinker,* April 10, 2011, http://www.americanthinker.com/2011/04/import_brazils_oil_policy_not.html

Cruz, Nancy, "Mexico: An Oil Nation in Crisis," *Council on Hemispheric Affairs*, Oct 22, 2009, http://www.coha.org/mexico-an-oil-nation-in-crisis/

Dominguez, Carlos, "Beyond Efficiency: The Politics of Investment Policies in the Oil Industry," *The Future of Oil in Mexico,* April 29, 2011, http://bakerinstitute.org/publications/EF-pub-DominguezEfficiency-04292011.pdf

Eller, Stacey, Hartley, Peter and Medlock, Kenneth, "Empirical Evidence on the Operational Efficiency of National Oil Companies," *The James A. Baker, III Institute for Public Policy, Rice University,* 2007, http://www.rice.edu/energy/publications/docs/NOCs/Papers/NOC_Empirical.pdf

Fraire, Leticia Armenta, "Breaking the cycle: Subsidies for transport fuels in Mexico," *Global Subsidies Initiative*, Nov 11, 2008, http://www.globalsubsidies.org/en/subsidy-watch/commentary/breaking-cycle-subsidies-transport-fuels-mexico

Goldstein, Andrea, "The Emergence of Multilatinas: The Petrobras Experience," *Universia Business Review*, 2010, http://ubr.universia.net/pdfs_web/25010-05.pdf

Gross, Daniel, "Norway vs. the Oil Curse," *Slate*, October 29, 2004, http://www.slate.com/articles/business/moneybox/2004/10/avoiding_the_oil_curse.html

Gue, Elliott, "Down Mexico Way: Oil and Politics South of the Border," *Seeking Alpha*, January 5, 2010, http://seekingalpha.com/article/180916-down-mexico-way-oil-and-politics-south-of-the-border

Hartley, Peter PhD and Medlock, Kenneth PhD, "The Revenue Efficiency of Pemex: A Comparative Approach," *The Future of Oil in Mexico*, April 29, 2011, http://bakerinstitute.org/publications/EF-pub-HartleyMedlockRevenue-04292011.pdf

http://www.nationalgeographic.com/educator-resources/oil-spills/map/gulf-oil/

Jane's Military and Security Assessments, "Natural Resources," Feb 16, 2011, http://jmsa.janes.com/JDIC/JMSA/documentView.do?docId=/content1/janesdata/sent/cacsu/mexis040.htm@current&backPath=/JDIC/JMSA

Kelemen, Jasmina, "A Band-aid Approach," *ICIS Chemical Business*, September 7, 2009, http://www.icis.com/Articles/2009/09/07/9243874/mexicos-pemex-seeks-to-stem-the-decline-in-oil-production.html

King, Byron, "Mexico's Crashing Oil Industry," *WhiskeyandGunpowder.com*, August 9, 2010, http://whiskeyandgunpowder.com/mexicos-crashing-oil-industry/

Krauss, Clifford, and Elisabeth Malkin, "Mexico Oil Politics Keeps Riches Just Out of Reach,"
The New York Times, March 8, 2010,
http://www.nytimes.com/2010/03/09/business/global/09pemex.html

Lan, Megan, Marcelo Silva, and Renzo Weber, "The Mexican Oil Dilemma: Refining Pemex,"
The Wharton School of the University of Pennsylvania, April 20, 2009,
http://knowledge.wharton.upenn.edu/article.cfm?articleid=2222

Little, Amanda, "Pumped Up: Chevron Drills Down 30,000 Feet to Tap Oil-Rich Gulf of
Mexico," *Wired*, August 21, 2007, http://www.wired.com/cars/energy/magazine/15-
09/mf_jackrig?currentPage=all

Mares, David PhD, "Oil Policy Reform in Resource Nationalist States: Lessons for Mexico," *The
Future of Oil in Mexico*, April 29, 2011, http://bakerinstitute.org/publications/EF-pub-
MaresLessons-04292011.pdf

Maurer, Noel, "The Empire Struck Back: The Mexican Oil Expropriation of 1938
Reconsidered," *Harvard Business School*, October 13, 2011.
http://www.hbs.edu/research/pdf/10-108.pdf

Morton, G.R, "Cantarell, The Second Largest Oil Field in the World is Dying," *Energy Bulletin*,
August 18, 2004, http://www.energybulletin.net/node/1651

O'Boyle, Michael, and Noel Randewich, "Mexico takes economic gamble to keep fuel cheap,"
Reuters, May 29, 2008, http://www.reuters.com/article/2008/05/29/us-mexico-economy-
idUSN2944639820080529

O'Keefe, Brian, and Doris Burke, "Petrobras: The next oil colossus," *CNNMoney*, March 8,
2011, http://features.blogs.fortune.cnn.com/2011/03/08/petrobras-the-next-oil-colossus/

Pemex, "Investor Relations," March 8, 2011,
http://contratos.pemex.com/portal/files/content/20110308cmg.pdf.

PennEnergy, "Pemex Looks at US Refining Market as Domestic Gasoline Demand Surges,"
March 1, 2011,
http://www.pennenergy.com/index/articles/newsdisplay/1376607740.html

Ros, Jaime, "The Macroeconomic Consequences of Falling Oil Revenues in Mexico: A Looming
Crisis or a Mixed Blessing?" *The Future of Oil in Mexico*, April 29, 2011,
http://bakerinstitute.org/publications/EF-pub-RosMacroeconomic-04292011.pdf

Ryggvik, Helge, "The Norwegian Oil Experience: A toolbox for managing resources?" *Oslo:
University of Oslo*, 2010, http://www.sv.uio.no/tik/forskning/publikasjoner/tik-
artikkelserie/Ryggvik.pdf

Sanati, Cyrus, "Mexican oil may not be worth it," *CNNMoney,* Dec 9, 2010, http://money.cnn.com/2010/12/09/news/international/Mexico_oil.fortune/index.htm

Smolski, Andrew, "PEMEX and the long road to privatization," *Oilprice.com*, July 20, 2011, http://oilprice.com/Energy/Energy-General/PEMEX-and-the-long-road-to-privatization.html

Talwani, Manik PhD, "Oil and Gas in Mexico: Geology, Production Rates and Reserves," *The Future of Oil in Mexico,* April 29, 2011, http://bakerinstitute.org/publications/EF-pub-TalwaniGeology-04292011.pdf

The Economist, "How many Mexicans does it take to drill an oil well?" October 1, 2009, http://www.economist.com/node/14548839

The Oil Drum, "Cantarell's loss is Ku-Maloob-Zaap's (KMZ) gain," February 7, 2007, http://www.theoildrum.com/node/2247

Thomson, Adam, "Pemex issues private oil-production contracts," *Financial Times,* August 18, 2011, http://www.ft.com/cms/s/0/959c20ca-c9d2-11e0-b88b-00144feabdc0.html#axzz1bdP2n3Gb

Triedman, Julie, "Petrobras Stock Offering Raises $67 Billion, Setting New Record," *The Am Law Daily*, Sept 24, 2010, http://www.law.com/jsp/tal/PubArticleFriendlyTAL.jsp?id=1202472570962

Universidad Nacional Autonoma De Mexico, 2005, http://www.juridicas.unam.mx/infjur/leg/constmex/pdf/consting.pdf

U.S. Department of Energy, "Petroleum & Other Liquids," June 24, 2011, http://www.eia.gov/dnav/pet/pet_pnp_cap1_dcu_nus_a.htm.

U.S. Energy Information Administration, Crude Oil and Petroleum Imports Top 15 Countries, 2011 Import Highlights, September 29, 2011, http://205.254.135.24/pub/oil_gas/petroleum/data_publications/company_level_imports/current/import.html

Wall, Allan, "PEMEX Fritters Away Mexico's Oil Wealth. Closing the Borders Would Help," *Memo from Mexico, V-Dare.com*, May 1, 2008, http://www.vdare.com/articles/memo-from-mexico-by-allan-wall-61.

Weedan, Scott, "Mexico Seeks Reserves in Deepwater Gulf," *E&P,* Aug 15, 2011, http://www.epmag.com/2011/August/item87111.php

Wood, Duncan, "The Outlook for Energy Reform in Latin America," *Woodrow Wilson International Center for Scholars*, March 2010, http://www.wilsoncenter.org/publication/the-outlook-for-energy-reform-latin-america